WEATHER MAKES THEM MOVE

GOOSE MIGRATION

by Rachel Rose

Consultant: Beth Gambro
Reading Specialist, Yorkville, Illinois

BEARPORT
PUBLISHING

Minneapolis, Minnesota

Teaching Tips

Before Reading

- Look at the cover of the book. Discuss the picture and the title.
- Ask readers to brainstorm a list of what they already know about geese. What can they expect to see in this book?
- Go on a picture walk, looking through the pictures to discuss vocabulary and make predictions about the text.

During Reading

- Read for purpose. Encourage readers to think about goose movement as they are reading.
- Ask readers to look for the details of the book. Why do geese migrate?
- If readers encounter an unknown word, ask them to look at the sounds in the word. Then, ask them to look at the rest of the page. Are there any clues to help them understand?

After Reading

- Encourage readers to pick a buddy and reread the book together.
- Ask readers to name a reason geese move. Find a page that tells about this thing.
- Ask readers to write or draw something they learned about goose migration.

Credits:

Cover and title page, © shaftinaction/Adobe Stock, © Rick/Adobe Stock; 3, © zennie/iStock; 4–5, © Symmetry Images/iStock; 6–7, © Emerson Gifford/Shutterstock; 9, © Ivan Kuzmin/Adobe Stock; 10–11, © Schuchart/Shutterstock; 13, © Dennis W Donohue/Shutterstock; 14–15, © Zachary Dobson/iStock; 17, © Milan/Adobe Stock; 18–19, © MWolskyPhoto/iStock; 20–21, © RCKeller/iStock; 22T, © Matthew Jolley/Adobe Stock; 22B, © jnjhuz/Adobe Stock; 23TL, © Michael Mamoon/Adobe Stock; 23TR, © BrianLasenby/iStock; 23BL, © Pavliha/iStock; 23BR, © MikeLane45/iStock.

Library of Congress Cataloging-in-Publication Data

Names: Rose, Rachel, 1968- author.
Title: Goose migration / by Rachel Rose.
Description: Minneapolis, Minnesota : Bearport Publishing Company, [2024] |
  Series: Weather makes them move | Includes bibliographical references
  and index.
Identifiers: LCCN 2022059196 (print) | LCCN 2022059197 (ebook) | ISBN
  9798888220658 (library binding) | ISBN 9798888222638 (paperback) | ISBN
  9798888223802 (ebook)
Subjects: LCSH: Geese--Migration--Juvenile literature. | Geese--Seasonal
  distribution--Juvenile literature.
Classification: LCC QL696.A52 R665 2024 (print) | LCC QL696.A52 (ebook) |
  DDC 598.4/171568--dc23/eng/20221212
LC record available at https://lccn.loc.gov/2022059196
LC ebook record available at https://lccn.loc.gov/2022059197

Copyright © 2024 Bearport Publishing Company. All rights reserved. No part of this publication may be reproduced in whole or in part, stored in any retrieval system, or transmitted in any form or by any means, electronic, mechanical, photocopying, recording, or otherwise, without written permission from the publisher.

For more information, write to Bearport Publishing, 5357 Penn Avenue South, Minneapolis, MN 55419.

Contents

Time to Fly 4

On the Move! 22

Glossary 23

Index 24

Read More 24

Learn More Online 24

About the Author 24

Time to Fly

It is almost winter.

The ground is getting cold.

It is time for geese to move.

Where will they go?

5

There are many kinds of geese.

During the summer, some geese live in Canada.

These Canada geese eat mostly plants.

7

As winter comes, it gets cold.

The ground **freezes**.

Plants stop growing.

It is hard for the geese to find food.

9

So, they fly south where it is warmer.

The birds **travel** in groups called **flocks**.

They move in a V shape.

The geese fly fast.

Soon, they reach the middle of the United States.

Some even fly as far as Mexico.

Canada geese have found a warmer spot.

They make winter homes.

Here, there is lots of food to eat.

When spring comes, it gets warmer in Canada.

The geese can go back home.

They fly to the same place every year.

Once there, the geese have babies.

The babies learn how to fly.

By fall, the young geese are ready to head south.

Every year, Canada geese go on this **journey**.

Weather really makes them move!

On the Move!

Migration (mye-GRAY-shuhn) is when animals move from one place to another. Often, they travel far. Let's learn more about Canada goose migration!

Canada geese fly south in September or October. They fly north in April or May.

The birds can travel more than 1,000 miles (1,600 km) in a single day.

Glossary

flocks groups that geese live and travel in

freezes gets so cold that liquid becomes ice

journey a long trip

travel to move from one place to another

Index

babies 19
Canada 6, 16
food 8, 14
freeze 8
plants 6, 8
south 10, 19, 22
United States 12

Read More

Hansen, Grace. *Canada Goose Migration (Animal Migration).* Minneapolis: Abdo Kids Jumbo, 2021.

Matthews, Colin. *Canada Goose Poop or Duck Poop? (The Scoop on Poop!).* New York: Gareth Stevens Publishing, 2020.

Learn More Online

1. Go to **www.factsurfer.com** or scan the QR code below.
2. Enter "**Goose Migration**" into the search box.
3. Click on the cover of this book to see a list of websites.

About the Author

Rachel Rose lives in California, where there are a lot of geese. Her pup, Sandy, loves to eat goose poop. *Yuck!*